SACREDSPACE

for Lent 2010

SACREDSPACE

for Lent 2010

from the website www.sacredspace.ie

Jesuit Communication Centre, Ireland

ave maria press AMP notre dame, indiana

acknowledgment

The Publisher would like to thank Piaras Jackson, S.J., and Alan McGuckian, S.J., for their kind assistance in making this book possible. Correspondence with the Sacred Space team can be directed to feedback@sacredspace.ie where comments or suggestions relating to the book or to www.sacredspace.ie will always be welcome.

Unless otherwise noted, the Scripture quotations contained herein are from the *New Revised Standard Version* Bible, copyright © 1989 by the Division of Christian Education of the National Council of the Churches of Christ in the United States of America. Used by permission. All rights reserved.

Published under license from Michelle Anderson Publishing Pty Ltd., in Australia.

Founded in 1865, Ave Maria Press is a ministry of the Indiana Province of Holy Cross.

www.avemariapress.com

ISBN-10: 1-59471-222-0   ISBN-13: 978-1-59471-222-7

Cover design by Andy Wagoner.

Text design by K. Hornyak.

Printed and bound in the United States of America.

how to use this book

During this Lenten season, we invite you to make a sacred space in your day. Spend ten minutes praying here and now, wherever you are, with the help of a prayer guide and scripture chosen specially for each day. Every place is a sacred space so you may wish to have this little book available at any time or place during the course of the day . . . in your desk at work, while traveling, on your bedside table, in your purse or jacket pocket. . . . Remember that God is everywhere, all around us, constantly reaching out to us, even in the most unlikely situations. When we know this, and with a bit of practice, we can pray anywhere.

The following pages will guide you through a session of prayer stages.

Something to think and pray about each day
this week

The Presence of God

Freedom

Consciousness

The Word (leads you to the daily Lenten scripture and provides help with the text)

Conversation

Conclusion

It is most important to come back to these pages
each day of the week as they are an integral part
of each day's prayer and lead to the scripture and
inspiration points.

Although written in the first person, the
prayers are for "doing" rather than for reading
out. Each stage is a kind of exercise or meditation
aimed at helping you to get in touch with God
and God's presence in your life.

We hope that you will join the many people around the world praying with us in our sacred space.

The Presence of God

Bless all who worship you, almighty God,
from the rising of the sun to its setting:
from your goodness enrich us,
by your love inspire us,
by your Spirit guide us,
by your power protect us,
in your mercy receive us,
now and always.

Something to think and pray about each day this week:

The Invitation to Freedom

We are at the start of Lent, the time of the year when the church invites us to test our freedom and to question the notion: I can take it or leave it alone. Try that with grumbling, drunkenness, talking about yourself, stealing, gambling, or other habits that diminish our freedom. What habits make you hard to live with? Lent is about regaining control of our own lives, especially in those areas that damage other people. We don't admire those whose appetites or habits lead them by the nose. Nearly all of us have habits, or even addictions, that keep us from God and harm both ourselves and others. These seven weeks before Easter help us to focus our energy on improving.

The Presence of God

For a few moments, I think of God's veiled presence in things:
in the elements, giving them existence;
in plants, giving them life; in animals, giving them sensation;
and finally, in me, giving me all this and more, making me a temple, a dwelling-place of the Spirit.

Freedom

God is not foreign to my freedom.
Instead the Spirit breathes life into my most intimate desires,
gently nudging me toward all that is good.

I ask for the grace to let myself be enfolded by the Spirit.

Consciousness

Knowing that God loves me unconditionally,
I can afford to be honest about how I am.
How has the last day been, and how do I feel now?
I share my feelings openly with the Lord.

The Word

The word of God comes down to us through the scriptures.
May the Holy Spirit enlighten my mind and my heart to respond to the gospel teachings.
(Please turn to your scripture on the following pages. Inspiration points are there should you need them. When you are ready, return here to continue.)

Conversation

How has God's Word moved me? Has it left me cold?

Has it consoled me or moved me to act in a new way?

I imagine Jesus standing or sitting beside me, I turn and share my feelings with him.

Conclusion

Glory be to the Father, and to the Son, and to the Holy Spirit,

As it was in the beginning, is now, and ever shall be,

World without end. Amen

Wednesday 17th February,
Ash Wednesday   **Psalm 51:1–10**

Have mercy on me, O God, according to your steadfast love; according to your abundant mercy blot out my transgressions. Wash me thoroughly from my iniquity, and cleanse me from my sin. For I know my transgressions, and my sin is ever before me. Against you, you alone, have I sinned, and done what is evil in your sight, so that you are justified in your sentence and blameless when you pass judgment. Indeed, I was born guilty, a sinner when my mother conceived me. You desire truth in the inward being; therefore teach me wisdom in my secret heart. Purge me with hyssop, and I shall be clean; wash me, and I shall be whiter than snow. Let me hear joy and gladness; let the bones that you have crushed rejoice. Hide your face from my sins, and blot out all my iniquities. Create in me a clean heart, O God, and put a new and right spirit within me.

- "Put a new and right spirit within me." Have I the courage to trust myself to this profound, Godly love that would take my broken sinfulness and recreate me with a clean heart?

- How does this affect me as I begin my Lenten journey?

Thursday 18th February   Luke 9:22–25

Jesus said to his disciples: "The Son of Man must undergo great suffering, and be rejected by the elders, chief priests, and scribes, and be killed, and on the third day be raised." Then he said to them all, "If any want to become my followers, let them deny themselves and take up their cross daily and follow me. For those who want to save their life will lose it, and those who lose their life for my sake will save it. What does it profit them if they gain the whole world, but lose or forfeit themselves?"

- Jesus gives advice that is both spiritually and psychologically sound. We hold in high esteem those who give their lives for a worthy cause, even to the point of losing their own.

- Am I spending most of my time winning what is unimportant—position, status, wealth—while turning a deaf ear to those around me? Am I "existing" or "living"?

Friday 19th February   Matthew 9:14–15

Then the disciples of John came to him, saying, "Why do we and the Pharisees fast often, but your disciples do not fast?" And Jesus said to them, "The wedding guests cannot mourn as long as the bridegroom is with them, can they? The days will come when the bridegroom is taken away from them, and then they will fast."

- Lord, you used a lovely image for your time with us: a honeymoon period, a week when the bride and groom kept open house and relished the joy of new love.

- To be with you then was to know that the world is young and full of hope, while realizing that the honeymoon joy will not last forever.

Saturday 20th February   Luke 5:27–32

After this he went out and saw a tax collector named Levi, sitting at the tax booth; and he said to him, "Follow me." And he got up, left everything, and followed him. Then Levi gave a great banquet for him in his house; and there was a large crowd of tax collectors and others sitting at the table with them. The Pharisees and their scribes were complaining to his disciples, saying, "Why do you eat and drink with tax collectors and sinners?" Jesus answered, "Those who are well have no need of a physician, but those who are sick; I have come to call not the righteous but sinners to repentance."

- Who today would be in Matthew's position, hated and despised by the public? Not the tax collectors: it is quite respectable now to work for the Internal Revenue Service. The media parades different hate-objects for us today: drug dealers, rapists, pedophiles.

- You would sit with them, Lord. They too need your grace.

Something to think and pray about each day this week:

The Taste of Life

When Ignatius Loyola was recovering after breaking his leg in battle, he used to enjoy the romances they gave him to read; but he found that their aftertaste was empty and unsatisfying. When he read the gospels, the aftertaste was of solid food, something he could live on. He learned to discern the aftertaste of experiences. That is the way the Holy Spirit can shape our lives. It means listening to our hearts to discover the path of God and of the Holy Spirit through us, and to recognize what blocks we place, consciously or unconsciously, to God's work in us.

The Presence of God

For a few moments, I think of God's veiled
presence in things:
in the elements, giving them existence;
in plants, giving them life; in animals, giving
them sensation;
and finally, in me, giving me all this and more,
making me a temple, a dwelling-place of the
Spirit.

Freedom

God is not foreign to my freedom.
Instead the Spirit breathes life into my most
intimate desires,
gently nudging me toward all that is good.
I ask for the grace to let myself be enfolded by
the Spirit.

Consciousness

Knowing that God loves me unconditionally,
I can afford to be honest about how I am.

How has the last day been, and how do I feel now? I share my feelings openly with the Lord.

The Word

I take my time to read the Word of God, slowly, a few times, allowing myself to dwell on anything that strikes me. (Please turn to your scripture on the following pages. Inspiration points are there should you need them. When you are ready, return here to continue.)

Conversation

How has God's Word moved me? Has it left me cold?

Has it consoled me or moved me to act in a new way?

I imagine Jesus standing or sitting beside me, I turn and share my feelings with him.

Conclusion

Glory be to the Father, and to the Son, and to the Holy Spirit,

As it was in the beginning, is now, and ever shall be,

World without end. Amen

Sunday 21st February,
First Sunday of Lent   Luke 4:1–13

Jesus, full of the Holy Spirit, returned from the Jordan and was led by the Spirit in the wilderness, where for forty days he was tempted by the devil. He ate nothing at all during those days, and when they were over, he was famished. The devil said to him, "If you are the Son of God, command this stone to become a loaf of bread." Jesus answered him, "It is written, 'One does not live by bread alone.'" Then the devil led him up and showed him in an instant all the kingdoms of the world. And the devil said to him, "To you I will give their glory and all this authority; for it has been given over to me, and I give it to anyone I please. If you, then, will worship me, it will all be yours." Jesus answered him, "It is written, 'Worship the Lord your God, and serve only him.'" Then the devil took him to Jerusalem, and placed him on the pinnacle of the temple, saying to him,

"If you are the Son of God, throw yourself down from here, for it is written, 'He will command his angels concerning you, to protect you,' and 'On their hands they will bear you up, so that you will not dash your foot against a stone.'" Jesus answered him, "It is said, 'Do not put the Lord your God to the test.'" When the devil had finished every test, he departed from him until an opportune time.

- How do the temptations of Jesus speak to my life? Do the devil's false promises and manipulations ring a bell with me?

- How am I tempted to dominate and use the material gifts of the world around me?

- Does the realization of temptation in my life weigh me down?

Monday 22nd February   Matthew 25:31–40

"When the Son of Man comes in his glory, and all the angels with him, then he will sit on the throne of his glory. All the nations will be gathered before him, and he will separate people one from another as a shepherd separates the sheep from the goats, and he will put the sheep at his right hand and the goats at the left. Then the king will say to those at his right hand, 'Come, you that are blessed by my Father, inherit the kingdom prepared for you from the foundation of the world; for I was hungry and you gave me food, I was thirsty and you gave me something to drink, I was a stranger and you welcomed me, I was naked and you gave me clothing, I was sick and you took care of me, I was in prison and you visited me.' Then the righteous will answer him, 'Lord, when was it that we saw you hungry and gave you food, or thirsty and gave you something to drink? And when was it that we saw you a stranger and welcomed you, or naked and gave you clothing? And when was it that we saw you sick or in prison and visited you?' And the king will answer them, 'Truly I tell you, just as you did it to one of the least of these who are members of my family, you did it to me.'"

- Where are the hungry, the naked, the homeless who would call on me if they could reach me? Or have I so organized my life that the needy never impinge on me?

- Lord, you have made this the sole criterion of judgment. How will I measure up?

Tuesday 23rd February   Matthew 6:7–13

"When you are praying, do not heap up empty phrases as the Gentiles do; for they think that they will be heard because of their many words. Do not be like them, for your Father knows what you need before you ask him. "Pray then in this way: Our Father in heaven, hallowed be your name. Your kingdom come. Your will be done, on earth as it is in heaven. Give us this day our daily bread. And forgive us our debts, as we also have forgiven our debtors. And do not bring us to the time of trial, but rescue us from the evil one."

- I need to be an adult, and a disciple of Jesus, before I can pray like this. In the Our Father I glorify God in the first three petitions, and then beg for my own needs, for bread, for forgiveness, and for removal from temptation.

- Let me pray it slowly, plumbing the depths in each phrase.

Wednesday 24th February   Luke 11:29–32

When the crowds were increasing, he began to say, "This generation is an evil generation; it asks for a sign, but no sign will be given to it except the sign of Jonah. For just as Jonah became a sign to the people of Nineveh, so the Son of Man will be to this generation. The queen of the South will rise at the judgment with the people of this generation and condemn them, because she came from the ends of the earth to listen to the wisdom of Solomon, and see, something greater than Solomon is here! The people of Nineveh will rise up at the judgment with this generation and condemn it, because they repented at the proclamation of Jonah, and see, something greater than Jonah is here!"

- You, Lord Jesus, are the sign of signs. Those who go seeking further wonders have not truly seen you. In you I find all that I need to be fully human and to find my destiny with God.

Thursday 25th February   Matthew 7:7–12

"Ask, and it will be given you; search, and you will find; knock, and the door will be opened for you. For everyone who asks receives, and everyone who searches finds, and for everyone who knocks, the door will be opened. Is there anyone among you who, if your child asks for bread, will give a stone? Or if the child asks for a fish, will give a snake? If you then, who are evil, know how to give good gifts to your children, how much more will your Father in heaven give good things to those who ask him! In everything do to others as you would have them do to you; for this is the law and the prophets."

- Jesus describes the setting: when we pray, we are not facing a begrudging God, who is easily irked by our requests. We are talking to a father, who wants to give all that is good for his child. The rabbis used to say: God is as near to his creatures as the ear to the mouth.

- Lord, I call on you with confidence, and I know you hear me.

Friday 26th February   **Matthew 5:20–24**

Jesus said to his disciples, "For I tell you, unless your righteousness exceeds that of the scribes and Pharisees, you will never enter the kingdom of heaven. You have heard that it was said to those of ancient times, 'You shall not murder'; and 'whoever murders shall be liable to judgment.' But I say to you that if you are angry with a brother or sister, you will be liable to judgment; and if you insult a brother or sister, you will be liable to the council; and if you say, 'You fool,' you will be liable to the hell of fire. So when you are offering your gift at the altar, if you remember that your brother or sister has something against you, leave your gift there before the altar and go; first be reconciled to your brother or sister, and then come and offer your gift."

• Lord, you are pulling me back from the action to the heart that prompts the action: from the good or bad deed to the love or anger that I allow to possess my heart. You want no part of my show of religion if it comes from a heart that is not at peace with those around me.

Saturday 27th February   Matthew 5:43–48

Jesus said to the disciples, "You have heard that it was said, 'You shall love your neighbor and hate your enemy.' But I say to you, Love your enemies and pray for those who persecute you, so that you may be children of your Father in heaven; for he makes his sun rise on the evil and on the good, and sends rain on the righteous and on the unrighteous. For if you love those who love you, what reward do you have? Do not even the tax collectors do the same? And if you greet only your brothers and sisters, what more are you doing than others? Do not even the Gentiles do the same? Be perfect, therefore, as your heavenly Father is perfect."

- The love to which Jesus calls us is not "passion" or "family feeling," but what the Greeks called *agape*, the habit of benevolence toward all, even those who see us with hostile eyes.

- Jesus admits that this sort of unselfish love is a high ideal, God-like in its perfection. It is the Holy Spirit who pours it out in our hearts.

Something to think and pray about each day this week:

Really Giving

When we are urged to be generous in these weeks of Lent, two phrases come to mind, the first from II Samuel 24. When King David wanted to buy Araunah's threshing floor in order to build an altar to God, and Araunah offered to give him the land for nothing, David replied: "I will not offer burnt offerings to the Lord my God that cost me nothing." The best giving is like the widow's mite: it twinges our heart and costs us something.

The second phrase is the old pastor's comment in *Babette's Feast*: "The only things we take with us from our life on earth are those which we have given away." It is a more blessed thing to give than to receive, and it brings greater happiness.

The Presence of God

I pause for a moment
and think of the love and the grace that God showers on me,
creating me in his image and likeness, making me his temple.

Freedom

Everything has the potential to draw forth from me a fuller love and life.
Yet my desires are often fixed, caught, on illusions of fulfillment.
I ask that God, through my freedom, may orchestrate
my desires in a vibrant loving melody rich in harmony.

Consciousness

In the presence of my loving Creator,
I look honestly at my feelings over the last day,
the highs, the lows, and the level ground.
Can I see where the Lord has been present?

The Word

God speaks to each one of us individually.
I need to listen to what he is saying to me.
(Please turn to your scripture on the following
pages. Inspiration points are there should you
need them. When you are ready, return here to
continue.)

Conversation

What feelings are rising in me
as I pray and reflect on God's Word?
I imagine Jesus himself sitting or standing
beside me,
and open my heart to him.

Conclusion

Glory be to the Father, and to the Son, and to the Holy Spirit,

As it was in the beginning, is now, and ever shall be,

World without end. Amen

Sunday 28th February,
Second Sunday of Lent   Luke 9:28–36

Now about eight days after these sayings Jesus took with him Peter and John and James, and went up on the mountain to pray. And while he was praying, the appearance of his face changed, and his clothes became dazzling white. Suddenly they saw two men, Moses and Elijah, talking to him. They appeared in glory and were speaking of his departure, which he was about to accomplish at Jerusalem. Now Peter and his companions were weighed down with sleep; but since they had stayed awake, they saw his glory and the two men who stood with him. Just as they were leaving him, Peter said to Jesus, "Master, it is good for us to be here; let us make three dwellings, one for you, one for Moses, and one for Elijah"—not knowing what he said. While he was saying this, a cloud came and overshadowed them; and they were terrified as they entered the cloud. Then from the cloud came a voice that said, "This is my Son, my Chosen; listen to him!" When the voice had spoken, Jesus was found alone. And they kept silent and in those days told no one any of the things they had seen.

- In this moment of "transfiguration," God the Father affirms Jesus for who he really is: "This is my Son, my Chosen". This must have been profoundly consoling. But, Jesus' being who he really was inevitably involved him going forward to do what he had to do.

- Can I allow the Father to affirm me for who I really am? Is there consolation for me?

- Does being who I really am hold any terrors for me?

Monday 1st March   Luke 6:36–38

Be merciful, just as your Father is merciful. "Do not judge, and you will not be judged; do not condemn, and you will not be condemned.

Forgive, and you will be forgiven; give, and it will be given to you. A good measure, pressed down, shaken together, running over, will be put into your lap; for the measure you give will be the measure you get back."

- Lord, I do not know enough to form a full judgment on those around me; it is not my business to pass sentence on them.

- But I know enough to forgive them, because I know my own frailty and how often I wish for forgiveness from others.

Tuesday 2nd March   Matthew 23:1–3, 6–9

Then Jesus said to the crowds and to his disciples, "The scribes and the Pharisees sit on Moses' seat; therefore, do whatever they teach you and follow it; but do not do as they do, for they do not practice what they teach. They love to have the place of honor at banquets and the best seats in the synagogues, and to be greeted with respect in the marketplaces, and to have people call them rabbi. But you are not to be called rabbi, for you have one teacher, and you are all students. And call no one your father on earth, for you have one Father—the one in heaven."

- Those are sweet titles, Rabbi or Father. It warms the heart to have the best seats and to be treated with respect.

- You are teaching me something, Lord, when these things change, when the pious are no longer exempt from public mockery. You are bringing me back from the complacency of the Pharisee to the state that you endured.

Wednesday 3rd March   Matthew 20:17–22

While Jesus was going up to Jerusalem, he took the twelve disciples aside by themselves, and said to them on the way, "See, we are going up to Jerusalem, and the Son of Man will be handed over to the chief priests and scribes, and they will condemn him to death; then they will hand him over to the Gentiles to be mocked and flogged and crucified; and on the third day he will be raised." Then the mother of the sons of Zebedee came to him with her sons, and kneeling before him, she asked a favor of him. And he said to her, "What do you want?" She said to him, "Declare that these two sons of mine will sit, one at your right hand and one at your left, in your kingdom." But Jesus answered, "You do not know what you are asking. Are you able to drink the cup that I am about to drink?'"

- This walk to Jerusalem is heavy with foreboding. Jesus tries to tell the Twelve of the fears that fill his soul: he will be betrayed by friends, delivered to his enemies; he will hear the death sentence read over him; he will suffer injustice, mockery, humiliation, insults; he will undergo the torture of scourging and finally face a horrific death on a gibbet.

- That is the cup you drank, Lord. If you ask me to share it, give me the strength.

Thursday 4th March   Luke 16:19–23

Jesus said to the Pharisees, "There was a rich man who was dressed in purple and fine linen and who feasted sumptuously every day. And at his gate lay a poor man named Lazarus, covered with sores, who longed to satisfy his hunger with what fell from the rich man's table; even the dogs would come and lick his sores. The poor man died and was carried away by the angels to be with Abraham. The rich man also died and was buried. In Hades, where he was being tormented, he looked up and saw Abraham far away with Lazarus by his side."

- There is a moral lesson here: the great danger of attending only to your own pleasures and not noticing those who are suffering.

- In a land where people were lucky to enjoy one good meal in the week, the rich man feasted sumptuously every day and did not notice Lazarus, who would have been glad even to receive crumbs.

- Lord, open my eyes. When I answer to you for my life, you will not ask in what neighborhood I lived, but you will ask how I treated my neighbor.

Friday 5th March   Psalm 104:24, 30–33

O Lord, how manifold are your works! In wisdom you have made them all; the earth is full of your creatures. When you send forth your spirit, they are created; and you renew the face of the ground. May the glory of the Lord endure forever; may the Lord rejoice in his works—who looks on the earth and it trembles, who touches the mountains and they smoke. I will sing to the

Lord as long as I live; I will sing praise to my God while I have being.

- Lord, give me this morning the heart of a poet and singer, to sing your praise and see your works—especially this precious planet you entrusted to us—with grateful, astonished eyes.

Saturday 6th March   Luke 15:11–24

Jesus told this parable: "There was a man who had two sons. The younger of them said to his father, 'Father, give me the share of the property that will belong to me.' So he divided his property between them. A few days later the younger son gathered all he had and traveled to a distant country, and there he squandered his property in dissolute living. When he had spent everything, a severe famine took place throughout that country, and he began to be in need. So he went and hired himself out to one of the citizens of that country, who sent him to his fields to feed the pigs. He would gladly have filled himself with the pods that the pigs were eating; and no one gave him anything. But when he came to himself he said, 'How many of my father's hired hands have bread enough and to spare, but here I am dying of hunger! I will get up and go to my father, and I will say to him, "Father, I have sinned against heaven and before you; I am no longer worthy to be called your son; treat me like one of your hired hands."' So he set off and went to his father. But while he was still far off, his father saw him and was filled with compassion; he ran and put his arms around him and kissed him. Then the son said to him, 'Father, I have sinned against heaven and before you; I am no longer worthy to be called your son.' But the father said to his slaves, 'Quickly, bring out a robe—the best one—and put it on him; put a ring on his finger and sandals on his feet. And get the fatted calf and kill it, and let us eat and celebrate; for this son of mine was

dead and is alive again; he was lost and is found!'
And they began to celebrate."

- In different cultures over the centuries God has
  been pictured in all sorts of images and imagina-
  tions. In this parable, we have Jesus' astonishing
  image. God is a fond father who does not stop
  his wastrel son from bringing shame on himself
  and the family; then he not only forgives him but
  also falls on his neck, interrupts his apology, and
  throws a big party to express his own joy.

- Dear Lord, whatever happens to me, let me never
  forget or doubt this picture of you.

Something to think and pray about each day this week:

Slow Food

Lent is a good time for thinking about meals: not so much about fish and fasting, as about making the effort—unusual now—to arrange family meals. There was a time when preparing a meal was a slow business, often seen as the main work of the mother of the house. When it was ready, the household gathered and shared the available food. No distractions—this is what we have been waiting for. It embodied the care and skill of the mother or of whoever prepared and cooked it. It was a time you did not miss, because you were hungry and because the action was here. You would feel out of it if you missed the coming together, no matter how rowdy or quarrelsome it might be. You would fight for your corner, and even if you were bested, you stayed at the table. Slow food made for better company.

The Presence of God
I reflect for a moment on God's presence around me and in me.
Creator of the universe, the sun and the moon, the earth,
every molecule, every atom, everything that is:
God is in every beat of my heart. God is with me, now.

Freedom
A thick and shapeless tree-trunk would never believe
that it could become a statue, admired as a miracle of sculpture,

and would never submit itself to the chisel of
the sculptor,

who sees by her genius what she can make of it.

(St Ignatius)

I ask for the grace to let myself be shaped by my
loving Creator.

Consciousness

Knowing that God loves me unconditionally,

I look honestly over the last day, its events and
my feelings.

Do I have something to be grateful for? Then I
give thanks.

Is there something I am sorry for? Then I ask
forgiveness.

The Word

I read the Word of God slowly a few times
over, and I listen to what God is saying to me.

(Please turn to your scripture on the following
pages. Inspiration points are there should you

need them. When you are ready, return here to continue.)

Conversation

What is stirring in me as I pray?
Am I consoled, troubled, left cold?
I imagine Jesus himself standing or sitting at my side,
and share my feelings with him.

Conclusion

Glory be to the Father, and to the Son, and to the Holy Spirit,
As it was in the beginning, is now, and ever shall be,
World without end. Amen

Sunday 7th March,
Third Sunday of Lent   Luke 13:1–9

A t that very time there were some present who told him about the Galileans whose blood Pilate had mingled with their sacrifices. He asked them, "Do you think that because these Galileans suffered in this way they were worse sinners than all other Galileans? No, I tell you; but unless you repent, you will all perish as they did. Or those eighteen who were killed when the tower of Siloam fell on them—do you think that they were worse offenders than all the others living in Jerusalem? No, I tell you; but unless you repent, you will all perish just as they did." Then he told this parable: "A man had a fig tree planted in his vineyard; and he came looking for fruit on it and found none. So he said to the gardener, 'See here! For three years I have come looking for fruit on this fig tree, and still I find none. Cut it down! Why should it be wasting the soil?' He replied, 'Sir, let it alone for one more year, until I dig around it and put manure on it. If it bears fruit next year, well and good; but if not, you can cut it down.'"

- Do I hear different voices of judgment in the passage? What do they spark in me? What about the gardener? What does he say?

- Is there a tendency towards harsh judgment in me—towards others or towards myself?

- Can I hear the voice of the gardener speaking within me?

Monday 8th March   Luke 4:24–30

And he said, "Truly I tell you, no prophet is accepted in the prophet's hometown. But the truth is, there were many widows in Israel in the time of Elijah, when the heaven was shut up three years and six months, and there was a severe famine over all the land; yet Elijah was sent to none of them except to a widow at Zarephath in Sidon. There were also many lepers in Israel in the time of the prophet Elisha, and none of them was cleansed except Naaman the Syrian." When they heard this, all in the synagogue were filled with rage. They got up, drove him out of the town, and led him to the brow of the hill on which their town was built, so that they might hurl him off the cliff. But he passed through the midst of them and went on his way.

- Jesus, speaking to his Jewish neighbors in Nazareth, is pointing to instances of God reaching out to the Gentiles, and the listeners are furious.

- How we cherish this illusion that we are the center of the universe, and that outsiders do not count! Unblinker me, Lord.

Tuesday 9th March   Matthew 18:21–35

Then Peter came and said to him, "Lord, if another member of the church sins against me, how often should I forgive? As many as seven times?" Jesus said to him, "Not seven times, but, I tell you, seventy-seven times. For this reason the kingdom of heaven may be compared to a king who wished to settle accounts with his slaves. When he began the reckoning, one who owed him ten thousand talents was brought to him; and, as he could not pay, his lord ordered him to be sold, together with his wife and children and all his possessions, and payment to be made. So the slave fell on his knees before him, saying, 'Have patience with me, and I will pay you everything.' And out of pity for him, the lord of that slave released him and forgave him the debt. But that same slave, as he went out, came upon one of his fellow slaves who owed him a hundred denarii; and seizing him by the throat, he said, 'Pay what you owe.' Then his fellow slave fell down and pleaded with him, 'Have patience with me, and I will pay you.' But he refused; then he went and threw him into prison until he would pay the debt. When his fellow slaves saw what had happened, they were greatly distressed, and they went and reported to their lord all that had taken place. Then his lord summoned him and said to him, 'You wicked slave! I forgave you all that debt because you pleaded with me. Should you not have had mercy on your fellow slave, as I had mercy on you?' And in anger his lord handed him over to be tortured until he would pay his entire debt. So my heavenly Father will also do to every one of you, if you do not forgive your brother or sister from your heart."

- A warlord begs foreign donors to bring water to his desert land; then he entertains journalists in his palace, with its six swimming pools. Like the unforgiving creditor in the gospel, he probably did not notice the inconsistency.

- Lord, I show understanding and sympathy with my own desires, but apply different standards to others. Can I look hard at my behavior? Will I find hypocrisy there?

Wednesday 10th March   Matthew 5:17–19

Jesus said to his disciples, "Do not think that I have come to abolish the law or the prophets; I have come not to abolish but to fulfill. For truly I tell you, until heaven and earth pass away, not one letter, not one stroke of a letter, will pass from the law until all is accomplished. Therefore, whoever breaks one of the least of these commandments, and teaches others to do the same, will be called least in the kingdom of heaven; but whoever does them and teaches them will be called great in the kingdom of heaven.

- Lord, you criticized the petty regulations that had been added to the law of God, and summed up the law and the prophets in the love of God and our neighbor. You were not turning your back on the past, but deepening our sense of where we stand before God: not as scrupulous rule-keepers, but as loving children.

Thursday 11th March   Jeremiah 7:23–28

But this command I gave them, "Obey my voice, and I will be your God, and you shall be my people; and walk only in the way that I command you, so that it may be well with you." Yet they did not obey or incline their ear, but, in the stubbornness of their evil will, they walked in their own counsels, and looked backward rather than forward. From the day that your ancestors came out of the land of Egypt until this day, I have persistently sent all my servants the prophets to them, day after day; yet they did not listen to me, or pay attention, but they stiffened their necks. They did worse than their ancestors did. So you shall speak all these words to them, but they will not listen to you. You shall call to them, but they will not answer you. You shall say to them: This is the nation that did not obey the voice of the Lord their God, and did not accept discipline; truth has perished; it is cut off from their lips.

- "The stubbornness of their evil will." Lord, I know what you mean by my heart hardening. I have felt that in the past, when I was unwilling to be open to the fact of my cruelty or ignoring others' needs. I harden into a selfish shell.

- Your heart remained loving in face of hostility and injustice. Open my heart to your love.

Friday 12th March   Mark 12:28–34

One of the scribes came near and heard them disputing with one another, and seeing that he answered them well, he asked him, "Which commandment is the first of all?" Jesus answered, "The first is, 'Hear, O Israel: the

Lord our God, the Lord is one; you shall love the Lord your God with all your heart, and with all your soul, and with all your mind, and with all your strength.' The second is this, 'You shall love your neighbor as yourself.' There is no other commandment greater than these." Then the scribe said to him, "You are right, Teacher; you have truly said that 'he is one, and besides him there is no other'; and 'to love him with all the heart, and with all the understanding, and with all the strength,' and 'to love one's neighbor as oneself,'—this is much more important than all whole burnt offerings and sacrifices." When Jesus saw that he answered wisely, he said to him, "You are not far from the kingdom of God." After that no one dared to ask him any question.

- From the wordy chapters of the Old Testament, Jesus picks out just two sentences, one from Deuteronomy and one from Leviticus, to give us a guide to life.

march 2010

- As I listen to his words in prayer, I can share the joy and enthusiasm of the scribe at this lovely simplicity.

Saturday 13th March Luke 18:9–14

He also told this parable to some who trusted in themselves that they were righteous and regarded others with contempt: "Two men went up to the temple to pray, one a Pharisee and the other a tax collector. The Pharisee, standing by himself, was praying thus, 'God, I thank you that I am not like other people: thieves, rogues, adulterers, or even like this tax collector. I fast twice a week; I give a tenth of all my income.' But the tax collector, standing far off, would not even look up to heaven, but was beating his breast and saying, 'God, be merciful to me, a sinner!' I tell you, this man went down to his home justified rather than the other; for all who exalt themselves will be humbled, but all who humble themselves will be exalted."

- Today, we might call the Pharisee a snob, a person who has "made it" and attributes all their good fortune to virtue and hard work. Behind this stance is an attitude, stated or unstated, that "I have done this by my own efforts; others can do it too if only they would work hard enough." There is no place for God there.

- Instead, Jesus presents us with the tax collector as the model for a prayerful attitude.

- I imagine myself in the Temple: with whom do I stand?

Something to think and pray about each day this week:

Christian Dreamtime

The Aboriginal community of Australia has its Dreamtime, a subconscious world of stories, memories, and images that have a powerful effect on our prayer, but are not easily documented in a way that would satisfy historians. The biblical book of Genesis is like the Australian Aboriginals' Dreamtime, full of parables about the creation of the world and its early history, parables that carry a profound truth for our human condition but do not relate to the careful researches of paleontologists. Those who have grown up in the faith find that they warm to certain non-theological images and practices. They light candles. They have their favorite saints. They are deeply moved by devotions such as novenas, the Camino de Santiago, fiestas and processions, which nurture their sense of the transcendent, of another world intersecting our existence. Just because the scholars cannot quote chapter and verse to prove their authenticity, we are not going to write off the Virgin of Guadalupe, or Our Lady of Lourdes, or the images of Padre Pio, or St. Jude's help in hopeless cases, or St. Anthony's help in finding what is lost. These are the treasures of our Dreamtime.

The Presence of God

In the silence of my innermost being,
in the fragments of my yearned-for wholeness,
can I hear the whispers of God's presence?
Can I remember when I felt God's nearness?
When we walked together and I let myself be
embraced by God's love.

march 2010

Freedom

There are very few people
who realize what God would make of them
if they abandoned themselves into his hands,
and let themselves be formed by his grace.
(St Ignatius)
I ask for the grace to trust myself totally to
God's love.

Consciousness

How do I find myself today?
Where am I with God? With others?
Do I have something to be grateful for? Then I
give thanks.
Is there something I am sorry for? Then I ask
forgiveness.

The Word

I take my time to read the Word of God, slowly,
a few times, allowing myself to dwell on anything
that strikes me. (Please turn to your scripture on

the following pages. Inspiration points are there should you need them. When you are ready, return here to continue.)

Conversation
Do I notice myself reacting as I pray with the Word of God?
Do I feel challenged, comforted, angry?
Imagining Jesus sitting or standing by me,
I speak out my feelings, as one trusted friend to another.

Conclusion
Glory be to the Father, and to the Son, and to the Holy Spirit,
As it was in the beginning, is now, and ever shall be,
World without end. Amen

Sunday 14th March,
Fourth Sunday of Lent   Luke 15:11–24

Then Jesus said, "There was a man who had two sons. The younger of them said to his father, 'Father, give me the share of the property that will belong to me.' So he divided his property between them. A few days later the younger son gathered all he had and traveled to a distant country, and there he squandered his property in dissolute living. When he had spent everything, a severe famine took place throughout that country, and he began to be in need. So he went and hired himself out to one of the citizens of that country, who sent him to his fields to feed the pigs. He would gladly have filled himself with the pods that the pigs were eating; and no one gave him anything. But when he came to himself he said, 'How many of my father's hired hands have bread enough and to spare, but here I am dying of hunger! I will get up and go to my father, and

I will say to him, "Father, I have sinned against heaven and before you; I am no longer worthy to be called your son; treat me like one of your hired hands.'" So he set off and went to his father. But while he was still far off, his father saw him and was filled with compassion; he ran and put his arms around him and kissed him. Then the son said to him, 'Father, I have sinned against heaven and before you; I am no longer worthy to be called your son.' But the father said to his slaves, 'Quickly, bring out a robe—the best one—and put it on him; put a ring on his finger and sandals on his feet. And get the fatted calf and kill it, and let us eat and celebrate; for this son of mine was dead and is alive again; he was lost and is found!' And they began to celebrate.

- When I do a quick scan of this story, where does my gaze lie? Is it on the abandonment, the dream gone sour, the degradation and squalor? Or, do I go straight to the picture of the father scanning the horizon, the compassion, the reconciliation and the forgiveness?

* My spontaneous inclination might tell me something about what I need to learn from this scripture.

* Where am I in my journey? Am I walking out the door? Am I in a foreign land? Or am I on the way home?

Monday 15th March   John 4:46b–50

Now there was a royal official whose son lay ill in Capernaum. When he heard that Jesus had come from Judea to Galilee, he went and begged him to come down and heal his son, for he was at the point of death. Then Jesus said to him, "Unless you see signs and wonders you will not believe." The official said to him, "Sir, come down before my little boy dies." Jesus said to him, "Go; your son will live." The man believed the word that Jesus spoke to him and started on his way.

- Jesus' first response seems harsh, even cynical: "Unless you see signs and wonders you will not believe." But the official doesn't seem to notice: "Sir, come down before my little boy dies."

- Jesus tested his faith further, but the man "believed the word that Jesus spoke to him." He went home to his son, without Jesus.

- Lord, teach me to have faith that you are with me always.

Tuesday 16th March   John 5:1–9

After this there was a festival of the Jews, and Jesus went up to Jerusalem. Now in Jerusalem by the Sheep Gate there is a pool, called in Hebrew Beth-zatha, which has five porticoes. In these lay many invalids—blind, lame, and paralyzed. One man was there who had been ill for thirty-eight years. When Jesus saw him lying there and knew that he had been there a long time, he said to him, "Do you want to be made well?" The sick man answered him, "Sir, I have no one to put me into the pool when the water is stirred up; and while I am making my way, someone else steps down ahead of me." Jesus said to him, "Stand up, take your mat and walk." At once the man was made well, and he took up his mat and began to walk.

- Jesus asks an intriguing question: Do you want to be made well? He knew the strength of habit and inertia: When you have been an invalid for thirty-eight years, a cure will impose responsibilities and make demands that some sick people might shy from.

- Lord, you ask me if I want to change, to go beyond my present state. Give me the strength to make the break.

Wednesday 17th March,
St. Patrick   Luke 10:1–2

After this the Lord appointed seventy others and sent them on ahead of him in pairs to every town and place where he himself intended to go. He said to them, "The harvest is plentiful, but the laborers are few; therefore ask the Lord of the harvest to send out laborers into his harvest."

- Jesus moved from the organized religion of the synagogue to preaching on the shore of the lake and wherever people gathered. St. Patrick did the same, talking to the Irish on hillsides and at river-crossings.

- The Good News cannot be organized into a neat institutional slot with its own buildings and officials. If I carry the sense of God's love with me, I will spread good news wherever I go.

Thursday 18th March   John 5:44–47

Jesus said to the Jews, "How can you believe when you accept glory from one another and do not seek the glory that comes from the one who alone is God? Do not think that I will accuse you before the Father; your accuser is Moses, on whom you have set your hope. If you believed Moses, you would believe me, for he wrote about me. But if you do not believe what he wrote, how will you believe what I say?"

- This reading reflects the age-old struggle between God and his chosen people, the Jews. It says something to us too: "How can you believe, who receive glory from one another, and do not seek the glory that comes from the only God?"

- Lord, I often hunger for ego-massage, for the good feeling when other people accept and approve of me. Do I make too much of it? Does it turn me from seeking you? Let me sniff the sweet air of flattery, but not inhale.

Friday 19th March,
St. Joseph   Psalm 89:1–2

I will sing of your steadfast love, O Lord, forever; with my mouth I will proclaim your faithfulness to all generations. I declare that your steadfast love is established forever; your faithfulness is as firm as the heavens.

- What inspires me in St. Joseph is his faithfulness, firm as the heavens. He was faithful to his fiancée though he could not understand her pregnancy, and he persevered as the faithful father of his family, supporting them through exile and danger.

- He was the quiet father whom many of us remember, there whenever he was needed, and a huge influence on Jesus.

Saturday 20th March   John 7:43–52

So there was a division in the crowd because of him. Some of them wanted to arrest him, but no one laid hands on him. Then the temple police went back to the chief priests and Pharisees, who asked them, "Why did you not arrest him?" The police answered, "Never has anyone spoken like this!" Then the Pharisees replied, "Surely you have not been deceived too, have you? Has any one of the authorities or of the Pharisees believed in him? But this crowd, which does not know the law—they are accursed." Nicodemus, who had gone to Jesus before, and who was one of them, asked, "Our law does not judge people without first giving them a hearing to find out what they are doing, does it?" They replied, "Surely you are not also from Galilee, are you? Search and you will see that no prophet is to arise from Galilee."

- Let me watch the movements in the crowd, and ask where I find myself. The chief priests are determined to silence Jesus as a threat to their authority. When Nicodemus quotes a legal principle at them, they ridicule him as soft. Yet as soon as the police hear the voice of the Jesus they have come to arrest, they fall under his spell: "Never has anyone spoken like this!"

- Lord, may I have the courage of Nicodemus and the police and be ready to stand against the crowd.

Something to think and pray about each day this week:

The Place of Prayer

Prayer is a spiritual place, a psychological place, a place where we go to get out of ourselves, a place created by and inhabited by our God. Whatever disciplines can help us to get to where God's reality can get at us, are those we should embrace.

Prayer isn't bending God's power in order to get things we want, or talking God into seeing things our way. It is whatever calls us to detach from our own self, from our own compulsions and addictions, from our own ego, from our own cozy space. We are all too trapped in our own places by virtue of the egocentricity of the human person.

In prayer the Spirit entices us outside our narrow comfort zone.

No wonder we avoid prayer: we have to change places, to move to a sacred space.

The Presence of God
In the silence of my innermost being,
in the fragments of my yearned-for wholeness,
can I hear the whispers of God's presence?
Can I remember when I felt God's nearness?
When we walked together and I let myself be
embraced by God's love.

Freedom
There are very few people
who realize what God would make of them
if they abandoned themselves into his hands,
and let themselves be formed by his grace.
(St. Ignatius)

I ask for the grace to trust myself totally to
God's love.

Consciousness

How do I find myself today?
Where am I with God? With others?
Do I have something to be grateful for? Then I
give thanks.
Is there something I am sorry for? Then I ask
forgiveness.

The Word

I take my time to read the Word of God,
slowly, a few times, allowing myself to dwell on
anything that strikes me. (Please turn to your
scripture on the following pages. Inspiration
points are there should you need them. When
you are ready, return here to continue.)

Conversation

Do I notice myself reacting as I pray with the
Word of God?
Do I feel challenged, comforted, angry?
Imagining Jesus sitting or standing by me,
I speak out my feelings, as one trusted friend to
another.

Conclusion

Glory be to the Father, and to the Son, and to
the Holy Spirit,
As it was in the beginning, is now, and ever
shall be,
World without end. Amen

Sunday 21st March,
Fifth Sunday of Lent John 8:2–11

Early in the morning Jesus came again to the temple. All the people came to him and he sat down and began to teach them. The scribes and the Pharisees brought a woman who had been caught in adultery; and making her stand before all of them, they said to him, "Teacher, this woman was caught in the very act of committing adultery. Now in the law Moses commanded us to stone such women. Now what do you say?" They said this to test him, so that they might have some charge to bring against him. Jesus bent down and wrote with his finger on the ground. When they kept on questioning him, he straightened up and said to them, "Let anyone among you who is without sin be the first to throw a stone at her." And once again he bent down and wrote on the ground. When they heard it, they went away, one by one, beginning with the elders; and Jesus was left alone with the woman standing before him. Jesus straightened up and said to her, "Woman, where are they? Has no one condemned you?" She said, "No one, sir." And Jesus said, "Neither do I condemn you. Go your way, and from now on do not sin again."

- I try to imagine this scene in the temple area with people coming and going. Suddenly there is a commotion. An angry crowd come to Jesus, parading a solitary woman in front of him.

- What is happening? Do I identify with any of the characters in the scene? Which one?

- How does Jesus react? How does his reaction touch me?

Monday 22nd March   Daniel 13:55–56; 60–62

Daniel said, "Indeed! Your lie recoils on your own head: the angel of God has already received from him your sentence and will cut you in half." He dismissed the man, ordered the other to be brought and said to him, "Son of Canaan, not of Judah, beauty has seduced you, lust has led your heart astray!" . . . Then the whole assembly shouted, blessing God, the Savior of those who trust in him. And they turned on the two elders whom Daniel had convicted of false evidence out of their own mouths. As the Law of Moses prescribes, they were given the same punishment as they had schemed to inflict on their neighbor. They were put to death. And thus, that day, an innocent life was saved.

- "Beauty has seduced you, lust has led your heart astray." Plenty of others—more men than women —have followed those old men in being led by lust into personal disaster.

- Incitement to lust is all around us. We can ask the Lord to guide us away from these temptations, and keep us centered on God.

Tuesday 23rd March   John 8:28–30

Jesus said to the Jews, "When you have lifted up the Son of Man, then you will realize that I am he, and that I do nothing on my own, but I speak these things as the Father instructed me. And the one who sent me is with me; he has not left me alone, for I always do what is pleasing to him." As he was saying these things, many believed in him.

- In a society that was used to public cruelty, death on a cross was both violent and a sign of public disgrace. It took centuries before Christians used the cross to represent their faith in the way we do today.

- Christ lifted on the cross says a great deal about God and humankind, about love and hate, and about sin and grace.

- What does the crucifix mean in my life? What is my role at the foot of the cross?

Wednesday 24th March John 8:31–32

Then Jesus said to the Jews who had believed in him, "If you continue in my word, you are truly my disciples; and you will know the truth, and the truth will make you free."

- "And the truth will make you free." Your listeners were Jews who faced the choice of following Jesus or remaining disciples of Moses.

- What will it cost me? What will I gain if I continue in the "word"?

- Can I start with the things about myself that I hide from and try to keep hidden from others?

Thursday 25th March,
Annunciation of the Lord Luke 1:26–29

In the sixth month the angel Gabriel was sent by God to a town in Galilee called Nazareth, to a virgin engaged to a man whose name was Joseph, of the house of David. The virgin's name was Mary. And he came to her and said, "Greetings, favored one! The Lord is with you." But she was much perplexed by his words and pondered what sort of greeting this might be.

- "Hail Mary, full of grace; *Ave Maria, gratia plena.*" As Mary heard that greeting, she grew shy and confused. I can never plumb the meaning of God made man, but that mantra, "Hail full of grace," engages my tongue while my mind tries to follow Mary in her joy and astonishment.

- She ponders the invitation in her heart, as she ponders later events in the life of her son. Then her response is from a full heart.

- Seat of Wisdom, teach me how to use my head and heart in a crisis.

Friday 26th March Jeremiah 20:10–13

For I hear many whispering: "Terror is all around! Denounce him! Let us denounce him!" All my close friends are watching for me to stumble. "Perhaps he can be enticed, and we can prevail against him, and take our revenge on him." But the Lord is with me like a dread warrior; therefore my persecutors will stumble, and they will not prevail. They will be greatly shamed, for they will not succeed. Their eternal dishonor will never be forgotten. O Lord of hosts, you test the righteous, you see the heart and the mind; let me see your retribution upon them, for to you I have committed my cause. Sing to the Lord; praise the Lord! For he has delivered the life of the needy from the hands of evildoers.

- Jeremiah spoke out on God's behalf. It cost him friends, led to attempts on his life, and to prison. He felt alone, betrayed, and angry.

- In the midst of these great trials he remained faithful. He begins feeling cut off and fearful; he ends in praise of the God who protects him from those who would do him harm.

- Let me take time to reflect on God's love for me and for all his people.

Saturday 27th March   **Ezekiel 37:21–23**

Thus says the Lord God: I will take the people of Israel from the nations among which they have gone, and will gather them from every quarter, and bring them to their own land. I will make them one nation in the land, on the mountains of Israel; and one king shall be king over them all. Never again shall they be two nations, and never again shall they be divided into two kingdoms. They shall never again defile themselves with their idols and their detestable things, or with any of their transgressions. I will save them from all the apostasies into which they have fallen, and will cleanse them. Then they shall be my people, and I will be their God.

- "They shall be my people, and I will be their God." This is an age-old promise; it expresses the mutual obligation on God and on his people.

- For Jews or Christians to see themselves as "special" is to miss the point. Along with the call to be faithful is a special responsibility to pass on to others the good news of God's covenant with his people.

- As I approach the time of Jesus' passion and resurrection, let me think about Abraham, Jeremiah, and Ezekiel and their faithful response to God.

- What comfort did Jesus draw from their examples?

march 28–april 3

Something to think and pray about each day this week:

Carrying the Cross

For those who pray with the Church, this is a painful week, the days in which we remember Jesus' passion and death. At one time, when a murder had been committed in a European village, neighbors were called to lay a hand on the crucifix and say they had no part in the murder. None of us can say that about Jesus' death. We all had a part in it. But we also share in his passion: we experience the cross in our lives, usually in the form of failure. Can I carry that cross as Jesus did, with love, as my share in redeeming the world, and with no bitterness?

The Presence of God
God is with me, but more,
God is within me, giving me existence.
Let me dwell for a moment on God's life-giving
presence
in my body, my mind, my heart,
and in the whole of my life.

Freedom
Many countries are at this moment suffering
the agonies of war.
I bow my head in thanksgiving for my freedom.
I pray for all prisoners and captives.

Consciousness
I remind myself that I am in the presence of the
Lord.
I will take refuge in His loving heart.
He is my strength in times of weakness.
He is my comforter in times of sorrow.

The Word

I read the Word of God slowly, a few times over,
and I listen to what God is saying to me. (Please
turn to your scripture on the following pages.
Inspiration points are there should you need
them. When you are ready, return here to continue.)

Conversation

How has God's Word moved me? Has it left
me cold?
Has it consoled me or moved me to act in a
new way?
I imagine Jesus standing or sitting beside me,
I turn and share my feelings with him.

Conclusion

Glory be to the Father, and to the Son, and to
the Holy Spirit,
As it was in the beginning, is now, and ever shall
be,
World without end. Amen

Sunday 28th March, Palm Sunday
of the Lord's Passion   Philippians 2:5–11

L et the same mind be in you that was in Christ Jesus, who, though he was in the form of God, did not regard equality with God as something to be exploited, but emptied himself, taking the form of a slave, being born in human likeness. And being found in human form, he humbled himself and became obedient to the point of death—even death on a cross. Therefore God also highly exalted him and gave him the name that is above every name, so that at the name of Jesus every knee should bend, in heaven and on earth and under the earth, and every tongue should confess that Jesus Christ is Lord, to the glory of God the Father.

• As Holy Week begins, I fix my eyes on Jesus. Simply mulling over the words of this beautiful early Christian hymn can help me appreciate the mystery of it.

Monday 29th March   **John 12:1–8**

Six days before the Passover Jesus came to Bethany, the home of Lazarus, whom he had raised from the dead. There they gave a dinner for him. Martha served, and Lazarus was one of those at the table with him. Mary took a pound of costly perfume made of pure nard, anointed Jesus' feet, and wiped them with her hair. The house was filled with the fragrance of the perfume. But Judas Iscariot, one of his disciples (the one who was about to betray him), said, "Why was this perfume not sold for three hundred denarii and the money given to the poor?" (He said this not because he cared about the poor, but because he was a thief; he kept the common purse and used to steal what was put into it.) Jesus said, "Leave her alone. She bought it so that she might keep it for the day of my burial. You always have the poor with you, but you do not always have me."

- Let me sit with this love-scene. Overjoyed to have Jesus as her guest, Mary produces her most precious possession, a fragrant perfume, and lavishes it upon Jesus' feet, then wipes them with her hair.

- It is a prodigal, unself-conscious act of love. She does not count the cost, but Judas does. Who am I more like, Mary or Judas?

- Teach me, Lord, to keep my eyes fixed on you.

Tuesday 30th March   **Isaiah 49:1–4**

Listen to me, O coastlands, pay attention, you peoples from far away! The Lord called me before I was born, while I was in my mother's womb he named me. He made my mouth like a sharp sword, in the shadow of his hand he hid me; he made me a polished arrow, in his quiver he hid me away. And he said to me, "You are my servant, Israel, in whom I will be glorified." But I said, "I have labored in vain, I have spent my strength for nothing and vanity; yet surely my cause is with the Lord, and my reward with my God."

- Like Israel, I was called by the Lord before I was even born.

- God has a plan for me, despite my sinfulness and weakness, my regular failings. "I will give you as a light to the nations, that my salvation may reach to the end of the earth."

- Can I make this plan my own?

Wednesday 31st March   Matthew 26:19–25

The disciples did as Jesus had directed them, and they prepared the Passover meal. When it was evening, he took his place with the twelve; and while they were eating, he said, "Truly I tell you, one of you will betray me." And they became greatly distressed and began to say to him one after another, "Surely not I, Lord?" He answered,

"The one who has dipped his hand into the bowl with me will betray me. The Son of Man goes as it is written of him, but woe to that one by whom the Son of Man is betrayed! It would have been better for that one not to have been born." Judas, who betrayed him, said, "Surely not I, Rabbi?" He replied, "You have said so."

- We wonder why Judas betrayed Jesus. Avarice? If so, he sold him cheap. More likely he was in some way disillusioned: He had expected Jesus to lead them to a messianic kingdom. Jesus was not the Christ that Judas expected him to be—too gentle and slow-moving. If so, he had tried to second-guess God.

- It is not Jesus who can be changed by us, but we who must be changed by Jesus.

Thursday 1st April,
Holy Thursday   John 13:12–16

After Jesus had washed their feet, had put on his robe, and had returned to the table, he said to them, "Do you know what I have done to you? You call me Teacher and Lord—and you are right, for that is what I am. So if I, your Lord and Teacher, have washed your feet, you also ought to wash one another's feet. For I have set you an example, that you also should do as I have done to you. Very truly, I tell you, servants are not greater than their master, nor are messengers greater than the one who sent them."

* Jesus kneeling with a towel round his waist is pointing to that aspect of Christianity in which there is no hierarchy, and the only rule is to meet the needs of others.

- On this feast of the Last Supper, John does not mention the Eucharist. He speaks only of service, one for another.

Friday 2nd April,
Good Friday   John 19:1–11

Then Pilate took Jesus and had him flogged. And the soldiers wove a crown of thorns and put it on his head, and they dressed him in a purple robe. They kept coming up to him, saying, "Hail, King of the Jews!" and striking him on the face. Pilate went out again and said to them, "Look, I am bringing him out to you to let you know that I find no case against him." So Jesus came out, wearing the crown of thorns and the purple robe. Pilate said to them, "Here is the man!" When the chief priests and the police saw him, they shouted, "Crucify him! Crucify him!" Pilate said to them, "Take him yourselves and crucify him; I find no case against him." The

Jews answered him, "We have a law, and according to that law he ought to die because he has claimed to be the Son of God." Now when Pilate heard this, he was more afraid than ever. He entered his headquarters again and asked Jesus, "Where are you from?" But Jesus gave him no answer. Pilate therefore said to him, "Do you refuse to speak to me? Do you not know that I have power to release you, and power to crucify you?" Jesus answered him, "You would have no power over me unless it had been given you from above; therefore the one who handed me over to you is guilty of a greater sin."

- St Peter Claver's life was spent in the holds of slave-ships with African victims who had no hope in this world. Out of that experience he used to say: The only book people should read is the story of the passion.

- A time comes to all of us to stretch out our hands as Jesus did, in passivity, unable to do anything with them: a time when God takes over, and our resistance folds. This is the hardest meditation; it touches a reality that in the long run we cannot escape.

- Love demands that we trust in a goodness and a life beyond our own. Lord, it is hard to contemplate. I pull away from the pain and injustice of this cross. Your love draws me back.

Saturday 3rd April,
Holy Saturday   John 19:25–30

Meanwhile, standing near the cross of Jesus were his mother, and his mother's sister, Mary the wife of Clopas, and Mary Magdalene. When Jesus saw his mother and the disciple whom he loved standing beside her, he said to his mother, "Woman, here is your son." Then he said to the disciple, "Here is your mother."

And from that hour the disciple took her into his own home. After this, when Jesus knew that all was now finished, he said (in order to fulfill the scripture), "I am thirsty." A jar full of sour wine was standing there. So they put a sponge full of the wine on a branch of hyssop and held it to his mouth. When Jesus had received the wine, he said, "It is finished." Then he bowed his head and gave up his spirit.

- "It is finished." The last words that Jesus speaks from the cross. He completed what he came to do, to show that God is love, and love conquers death.

- As Julian of Norwich wrote: " . . . the love that made him suffer all this—it passes as far beyond all his pains as heaven is above earth. For the passion was a deed done in time by the working of love; but the love is without beginning and is, and ever shall be, without . . . end."

april 4

Something to think and pray about each day this week:

The Easter Mystery

On the first Easter morning, the apostles and holy women did not see a ghost of Jesus. They saw him in the flesh, but in a different flesh, as the oak tree is different from the acorn that was its origin. We touch on the mystery of a body, not just Jesus' body but our own; a body which will express us at our best, will not dull our spirit with weariness and rebellion, but will express it with ease and joy. This is a mystery beyond our imagination, but it is the center of our faith. When we wish one another a happy Easter, we should take deep joy in the knowledge that the best part of us will cheat the grave. Our lives sometimes disguise that joy as weary bones, heavy flesh, and addled brains distract us. But our bodies already hold the seeds of resurrection. We are none of us mortal.

The Presence of God

To be present is to arrive as one is and open up to the other.
At this instant, as I arrive here, God is present waiting for me.
God always arrives before me, desiring to connect with me
even more than my most intimate friend.
I take a moment and greet my loving God.

Freedom

"In these days, God taught me
as a schoolteacher teaches a pupil" (St Ignatius).
I remind myself that there are things God has to teach me yet,

and ask for the grace to hear them and let them change me.

Consciousness

How am I really feeling? Light-hearted? Heavy-hearted?

I may be very much at peace, happy to be here. Equally, I may be frustrated, worried, or angry. I acknowledge how I really am. It is the real me that the Lord loves.

The Word

I take my time to read the Word of God, slowly, a few times, allowing myself to dwell on anything that strikes me. (Please turn to your scripture on the following pages. Inspiration points are there should you need them. When you are ready, return here to continue.)

Conversation

What feelings are rising in me
as I pray and reflect on God's Word?
I imagine Jesus himself sitting or standing
beside me
and open my heart to him.

Conclusion

Glory be to the Father, and to the Son, and to
the Holy Spirit,
As it was in the beginning, is now, and ever
shall be,
World without end. Amen

Sunday 4th April,

Easter Sunday John 20:1–9

Early on the first day of the week, while it was still dark, Mary Magdalene came to the tomb and saw that the stone had been removed from the tomb. So she ran and went to Simon Peter and the other disciple, the one whom Jesus loved, and said to them, "They have taken the Lord out of the tomb, and we do not know where they have laid him." Then Peter and the other disciple set out and went toward the tomb. The two were running together, but the other disciple outran Peter and reached the tomb first. He bent down to look in and saw the linen wrappings lying there, but he did not go in. Then Simon Peter came, following him, and went into the tomb. He saw the linen wrappings lying there, and the cloth that had been on Jesus' head, not lying with the linen wrappings but rolled up in a place by itself. Then the other disciple, who reached the tomb first, also went in, and he saw and believed; for as yet they did not understand the scripture, that he must rise from the dead.

- Can I imagine myself standing near to the tomb on the morning in question, before first light? I observe the comings and goings.

- How do the people look? First, the woman; can I see her face? What does she do next? Then two men . . .

- What has happened here?

DON'T MISS A DAY!

Order now for 2010

The Sacred Space series, inspired by the very popular, successful, and interactive website www.sacredspace.ie, offers a way to reflect and pray each day of the year.

ISBN: 9781594711947 / 384 pages

ISBN: 9781594711930 / 96 pages

ISBN: 9781594712227 / 128 pages

TO ORDER:
Call: 1-800-282-1865 · E-mail: avemariapress.1@nd.edu

 ave maria press® · Notre Dame, Indiana · www.avemariapress.com
E-mail: avemariapress.1@nd.edu • Ph: 1-800-282-1865 • Fax: 1-800-282-5681
A Ministry of the Indiana Province of Holy Cross

Availability subject to change.   Promo Code: FH8Ø6Ø917B6